HIMALAYA

HIMALAYA
Encounters with Eternity

77 color photographs and captions by Ashvin Mehta
Introduction by Maurice Herzog

Thames and Hudson

Photographs and captions © 1985 Ashvin Mehta
Text © 1985 Maurice Herzog

First published in the USA in 1985 by Thames and Hudson Inc.,
500 Fifth Avenue, New York, New York 10110
First paperback edition 1991

Library of Congress Catalog Card Number 90–70358

The text of Maurice Herzog has been translated
from the French by Jane Brenton.

Printed and bound in Hong Kong

Contents

Acknowledgments

Mr. Kantisen Shroff of Excel Industries Limited, Bombay, who advanced me an interest-free loan for this project, when its recovery had only the faintest of chances. He had the courage of his convictions to support me when many international organizations and publishers, and a well-known Indian industrialist, known for his innumerable donations to scientific and cultural projects, had all rejected my proposal.

my wife, for condoning and accepting my long absences from home – as long as six months in a year for five years, and for making my travels as comfortable as possible even when not accompanying me.

my elderly friend Mr. Umaprasad Mukherjee, a noted Bengali writer and the grand old man of trekking in Himalaya, for offering me valuable suggestions from time to time.

Mr H. C. Sarin of the Indian Mountaineering Foundation, for taking an active interest in the project since its inception and helping me in a number of ways.

Messrs Ratan Singh Chauhan (of the Nehru Institute of Mountaineering, Uttarkashi), Prem Singh Rawat (of Uttarkashi), and Khubram Thakur (of Manali) – all true gems among men – for accompanying me in my various trips as guide-cum-assistants and looking after me in the mountains. More than loyal and intelligent companions, they were deeply involved in my work.

Prime Minister Mrs Indira Gandhi and Mr Peter Drucker – both great lovers of nature and Himalaya, for viewing my work and recommending it, though unsuccessfully, to their respective publishers in Switzerland and the U.S.A.

Mr M. Ashraf, Asst. Director of Tourism (Trekking and Mountaineering), Government of Jammu & Kashmir, for helping me on my trips to Kashmir.

Survey of India, for supplying heights of certain places.

Mr Virbhadra Sinh, ex-Maharaja Rampur-Bushahar, and Chief Minister of Himachal Pradesh, for helping me in my trips to Spiti and Lahul.

Mr Lavkumar Khachar (of Rajkot), Mr Virendrakumar Gigoo and Mr Ravi Madan (both of Srinagar), Mr Harish Kapadia and other friends of the Himalayan Club, and many others who helped me in small but substantial ways in their various capacities, official or otherwise.

All those who were not only indifferent to the project but hindered it. I am indebted to them for presenting to me the other side of human behaviour. They put to test my norms of decent behaviour and truly made me large-hearted, patient and tolerant.

A personal statement
Ashvin Mehta

I was introduced to Himalaya quite suddenly and without any effort of my own. In my thoughts it was an area as remote as the Arctic, or even the moon, and existed only in books. Reading at the time for my master's degree in science, I was invited by Swami Anand, whom I barely knew, to join him in the mountains, where he spent almost eight months out of each year. More than thirty years have passed since that casual offer, and I have forgotten all the details of my maiden trip – not only to Himalaya but also to anywhere beyond 200 km. of my home town, Bombay. What I vividly remember, however, and expect to remember all my life, is the sight and touch of the swift and silent waters of the Ganga as it enters the plains from the Shivalik hills near Rishikesh; the fragrant pine forests scintillating with the brilliant orange and yellow and blue of minivets and Himalayan magpies; and, of course, the first view of snow mountains from the 3000-meter-high Deoban peak near Chakrata. The mountains seemed to float in the misty blue sky of early spring and were unbelievably high. Apart from clouds or stars, I had never seen anything on earth that high before. There was also an indefinable but very palpable presence, awesome and overwhelmingly beautiful at the same time. The experience was stunning, but I felt that I had known Himalaya for a long time. It was like meeting an old friend and not a stranger.

Thereafter, I trekked Himalaya at least every other year. With each trip my sensitivity grew, and found its haven in photography. In the mountains, I felt transported beyond technique and manipulation to the realm of art and creation. Gradually, the dichotomy between my profession and my first love, photography, took such frightening proportions that I had to leave my job. When I started as a free-lancer I knew that the price of freedom is total financial insecurity – especially when one shuns all 'commercial' work.

At a much younger age, even before I left my comfortable job, I realized that I was not cast in the mould of a mountaineer – a tough, bullish person out to match his wits and body against the vagaries of arctic weather, climbing and conquering forbidding peaks of the frozen wasteland. I was essentially an artist, a photographer, destined to decipher and interpret the poetry of the middle Himalaya (2000 to 5000 m), the playground of the seasons, alive with human, animal, and plant life. It is here, during spring, that every tree sings with birds, every blade of grass stirs with insects, and every flower hums with bees, when the multi-coloured carpet is laid out to welcome the 'king of seasons'. In the caves and monasteries of these mountains, Hindu and Buddhist spiritual aspirants and seers find inner sustenance in their long and lonely sojourns, and reach transcendental heights. For mountaineers, however, this middle Himalaya forms an 'approach march', whose only value lies in acclimatization of the body to high altitudes.

I am at a loss to portray through photography, which is essentially a visual art, the personal warmth and concern of many unknown people whom I met during my travels. Together they form an important aspect of Himalaya and show the inner fibre of a people nurtured by the greatest mountains on the face of our planet, and untouched by industrial society. In particular, I can never forget a Gujjar woman in Kashmir, who appeared from nowhere just to warn me against wild bears and advised me where to pitch my tents; another old woman in Garhwal who bade me a tearful farewell after a night's stay in her hut and stuffed all my pockets with plums; a poor Nepali farmer who shared with me – the seventh member of his family – the 30 square feet of dry ground under a leaky roof; a ten-year-old girl who lovingly snatched away my primulas and insisted that the first flowers of the season must be offered to the village deity; my youthful and exuberant guide in Kulu, who made me cross, without ice-axe or rope, slippery ice-tongues leading straight to the river flowing 1000 m. below; and a Buddhist pilgrim in Lahul, who bade me drink his only cup of Tibetan tea when I was wet, cold and frozen. I wish I could portray all this in my photographs!

According to Indian philosophy, the five elements of earth, water, fire, wind and sky (or space) are the Gods who form the limbs of the Formless. In this sense, my photography of nature and of Himalaya is an attempt to portray Him, and I have succeeded to the extent that I am able to capture the elements not merely as elements but as His limbs.

One may disapprove of or ignore such amalgamation of photography and vague religious sentiments. But if one pauses to consider the process of creativity in an artist, the final creation can rarely evoke eternity unless one was in touch with it at the time of genesis. It matters, therefore, whether one looks upon the elements as just elements or much more. A certain frame of mind can result in construction, and another – not a frame of mind but a state of communion – results in creation. All constructions are products of Time and vanish in Time, in spite of their glitter and apparent brilliance. The creations outlive Time and make both the viewer and the creator experience timelessness.

In my photography, I seek to celebrate the Gods, and through them sing of Him who has neither form nor age. I celebrate whether I am photographing the ethereal sunshine after a snow-storm in eastern Himalaya, or tender willows holding precariously on to sandy mountain slopes in Ladakh. I celebrate whether I am photographing a mother nursing her first-born under a huge bunyan tree, or a crafty sherpa eyeing trekkers from behind a stone wall in Khumbu.

8

The photographs in this book are a record of my celebration and of my encounter with eternity, or timelessness. In the actual experiencing of eternity, there is no form. The (human) form which experiences it and the form (Himalaya, in this case) which triggers the experiencing both dissolve in that moment. At a certain level of consciousness, and to one firmly bound to the senses and to the intellect, this can be a frightening and permanently disorientating experience. But at another level of existence, the same experience can result in beatitude, the supreme bliss. If my pictures of Himalaya can make the reader glimpse this eternity, or motivate him even to think of such an experience, I will be more than happy at having done my job well, and having been true to the heritage of the Mahatmans, or great souls, whom I consider my true ancestors.

Technical details

I believe all reputed brands of cameras are efficacious instruments for creative photography and that personal likes and dislikes are of emotional rather than technical significance. Pictures are not made by cameras and various accessories but by the 'seeing eye'. Yet, for the information of the curious reader, I may state that I used Asahi Pentax cameras – SP, SP II, SPF, F1000 and MX models, at various stages of the project, with 35 mm, 55 mm, 135 mm and 300 mm Pentax lenses, and UV, skylight, and polaroid filters. The film used was exclusively Kodachrome 25/64, and was developed in the Kodak Laboratory at Bombay, out of necessity rather than choice.

Introduction
Maurice Herzog

The West is becoming a soulless place. Its people are suffering progressively from the effects of frustration and restlessness, anxiety and outright fear – not to mention actual strife and warfare. Of course we take pride in this world of ours, which can justly boast of technological breakthroughs and an ever-increasing standard of material well-being. But a constant background of noise and images, speed, pollution and competition, are creating in what we choose to call the developed countries a type of human being who in no way corresponds to the ideal we dimly conceive of in the recesses of our consciousness, in our dreams and visions. The sicknesses and traumas afflicting our society are, alas, so deep-rooted and so numerous that we cannot dwell on them without being overcome by depression. To resign ourselves to them is even more debilitating. Who among us does not feel bitterness as we watch our young people sinking into lethargy, or else reacting in the opposite way and rushing blindly into the unknown, risking their mental and physical health?

Our world is changing with a rapidity beyond our control. The older ones among us can still recall a time when we lived by the light of candles, travelled on horseback and fetched water from communal wells. Today the circumstances of everyday life have been transformed by electricity and electronics, planes and satellites, television, nuclear power and information technology.

Surrounded on all sides by frenetic activity and confusion, men are obliged to develop split-second reflexes of self-defence or else become aggressors themselves, quick to strike. They have lost all feeling for the natural world. Far from appreciating calm and meditation, they are appalled by them. We are all of us slaves, yet we still dream of freedom, of rediscovering our true selves and our proper values.

Fortunately there are ways of escape. It is still possible to retreat for a while into the peace and quiet of a monastery, or to undertake a pilgrimage. And elsewhere in the world there do exist, even now, oases of sanity, places where ideas are still welcomed and the fundamental questions of life are being addressed. They are not merely repositories of old ideas, but breeding grounds of civilization and humanity. One of these rare places is the Himalayan mountain zone. It is set high above the earth, like an altar. It is both a sanctuary to retreat to, and a holy place. There, God still exists.

The poles are no more than points on the mechanical axis of our planet. Himalaya, however, is unique in its geographical location and, what is more, played a primordial role in the evolution of mankind. It is truly at the navel of the world.

The vast mountain chain never acted as a barrier between peoples. On the contrary, it was the source from which they all originated – just as springs bubble up on the hillsides and emerge later on as rivers.

According to the sacred ritual chants, or mantras, of the region, it was here that history began. All the races, peoples, languages and religions of the world emanated from the 'seat of the snows', Himalaya, a name enshrined in mythology.

If we are to believe the legend, human life came into existence in this great mountain complex that extends 2,500 kilometres across Asia, its peaks reaching up as though to defy the stars – fourteen of them attaining an altitude over 8,000 metres. Our planet is studded with sacred mountains that have looked to the skies for the gift of life. But the entreaties of Olympus, Fujiyama, Machu Picchu, Sinai, Ararat, and many others, were all in vain, in spite of miraculous interventions by the gods. No more successful were the artificial mountains built in an ultimate act of worship by the faithful – the pyramids of the Egyptians and Mayans, and the Tower of Babel.

It is, we are told, on Mount Kailas, home of Shiva, that man first appeared. (Science may dispute this – but science has a reputation for being blind.) Kailas is supposedly the geographical location of the mythological Mount Meru, cosmological centre of the world, which presides over the surrounding continents and seas. From its immeasurable heights the deity of contemplative asceticism looks down to act as a guide to humanity, and embraces the heavens. 'Calm as a cloud on the mountain, like a still lake without a breath of wind, like a lamp lit in a sheltered spot, so he stands in ecstasy, unbreathing.' So sang the poet Kalidasa when Shiva appeared to him on the summit of the holy mountain. The Buddhists too venerate Kailas and many pilgrims visit the spot in search of the wisdom and serenity preached by the Buddha.

The branches of the human family spread out in three directions, the blacks to the south, the yellow races to the north, and the white peoples to the west. All three prospered and multiplied. Thus the races were created.

This account of genesis also covers the original religions that satisfied the spiritual needs of our ancestors, Hinduism and Buddhism, as well as the later incarnations of the deity, or avatars, that gave rise to Christianity and Islam. There is no reference to Judaism even though the Middle East and the kingdom of Akkad are not far distant, and in fact migrations of population were more common than one might expect in those remote times.

Historical legends are robust and enduring. They gain in power from the poetic accretions of the mystics, obsessed with the need to bring everything into a unified and universal system; in this way a coherent body of dogma is slowly assembled.

From the various myths, we gather that a diaspora must have taken place, moving outwards from the epicentre of Mount Kailas. Buddhism spread to the north-east, in all its various manifestations: the different Canons, Tantrism and Lamaism in Tibet, and derivatives such as Confucianism in China and Shintoism in Japan. In the south-eastern region Hinduism enjoyed a virtually unchallenged superiority, in spite of the long and illustrious sovereignty of the Emperor-monk Asoka and his successors. And to the west, Islam became the true faith of its chosen peoples.

The various Asian languages, too, fit interestingly into this scheme. In Tibet they speak a tongue derived from Tibeto-Burmese, which has no etymological links with the Indo-European group of languages used to the south of Himalaya, but which does have certain parallels with Chinese. In the north of Pakistan we find Urdu (meaning 'army', and the origin of 'horde'), close to Hindi but written in Arabic script. To the west of the great chain the common language is Kashmiri, a development of Persian and Hindi, and to the south Hindi itself, to which Nepalese is closely related. In the extreme southern tip of the Indian sub-continent the Dravidian languages are spoken, notably Tamil; these bear very little resemblance to the Indo-European family of languages. Finally, to the west, we encounter Persian and Pharsee, words etymologically identical to 'Parthians' and 'Parsees' (who were disciples of Zoroaster driven out by Islam, settled to this day in the Bombay region).

The linguistic pattern is thus highly diverse. According to the myths, Mount Meru played the same role as the Tower of Babel. Perhaps we can assume that Shiva followed the example of the Old Testament God and ordered the confusion of tongues.

Sanskrit is in a category of its own. It is a language of the educated classes, although it is often confused with the primitive language, Vedic, spoken by the Aryans in 2000 BC. Sanskrit is really the creation of linguists and grammarians and was designed to express the subtle nuances of ideas. By a somewhat different process Pali became, in the time of the Buddha, a religious language. It was the vehicle by which Buddhism was spread through all of south-east Asia, notably in Burma, Campuchea and Indonesia.

Whatever the truth behind the mythological origins of the various languages, religions, civilizations and even racial types, one central historical fact is beyond dispute. Over the course of time they have tended to retreat back from western Asia into Himalaya, the last bastion against the Indo-Aryan invasions and the numerous others that followed.

The north of India has been a perennial battleground, ravaged time and time again by aggressors: by the Persian conquests of Darius, which led to the establishment of a satraphy in the Indus delta; by the invasions in the fourth century BC of Alexander the Great, who dreamed of reaching the Ganges, the 'frontier of the world'; the repeated attacks by the Greek kings of Bactria – one of whom, Menander, became a devout Buddhist; the Scythian incursions at the start of the Christian era, which also reached as far as the Ganges; the devastation in the fifth century by Barbarian hordes, of whom the Huns were the most famous. Later, from 775 to the end of the fourteenth century, the successive assaults of Islam and the bloody and destructive campaigns of Tamurlane laid waste the Indo-Gangetic plains. Ultimately, as these invaders in turn became civilized, a more settled society was established. In the sixteenth century, in order to consolidate their power base, the Islamic conquerors founded the Great Moghul Empire under Babur, direct descendant of Genghis Khan and Tamurlane. The dynasty produced the illustrious emperors Akbar (1556–1606) and Aurangzeb (1658–1707).

Population movement into Himalaya was further augmented by migrations from Tibet, by the Bhotias (the people of the land of Bon, ancient name of Tibet), among them the newari who settled in Nepal even before the start of the Christian era, and also the sherpas (the peoples of the east) and the Bhutanese.

Time and time again throughout history the great mountain chain has served to perpetuate and preserve human values. This is particularly true of the Kashmir region, which was later converted to Islam; Garhwal, in which are situated the sources of many of the sacred rivers; and Nepal, which has long been a centre of Hindu resistance, especially in the area around its capital, Kathmandu. In the face of the successive invasions that profoundly altered the ancient civilizations and the societies of the countries on which it borders, the Himalayan zone quite naturally became a place of sanctuary, protected as it was by the gods who dwelt in the mountains.

To understand these events fully, and trace the historical development of the region, it is helpful to have a broad outline of its geography. The word Himalaya derives from the Sanskrit 'hima' and 'alaya', meaning 'seat of the snows'. The massif is in the form of a shallow crescent with its open side facing towards the north. It erects a physical (although, as we know, not a demographic) barrier between the Indian sub-continent and the rest of Asia, specifically the Tibetan plateau. At each of its extremities it is flanked by a colossal pillar of rock that resembles a forbidding sentinel guarding the domain of the gods: to the west, the Nanga Parbat in Pakistan (8,125 metres) and to the east, the Namcha Barwa (7.756 metres) on the Tibeto-Chinese borders, in the northern region of the NEFA zone (North East Frontiers Agency), currently claimed by China.

In northern Himalaya, in Tibetan territory and directly above the western tip of Nepal, there stands the extraordinary 'water tower' of Mount Kailas, axis of the world. It is no more than 6,192 metres above sea level, while on the opposite side of the sacred Lake Manasarowar ('manas' means intellect), itself at an altitude of 4,490 metres, there is curiously enough a much higher peak, the Gurla Mandata (7,728 metres).

In or near these venerated mountains lie the sources of all the major rivers of Asia, or at least of southern Asia. First the Tsangpo, which flows eastwards along the Himalayan range, right through Tibet, before curling round the heights of Namcha Barwa. Taking the name of Brahmaputra (son of Brahma), it flows down over the plains of Assam and Bengal to disappear into the Ganges delta.

There is the Indus, which flows to the west and reaches Jammu and Kashmir by way of Ladakh. Not far from Srinagar, at the foot of Nun Kun (7,135 metres) is a famous place of pilgrimage, Amarnath, where the faithful come to prostrate themselves in front of a *linga* formed out of ice. After skirting Nanga Parbat, the great river goes down into the plains of Pakistan and debouches into the sea of Oman, which forms part of the Indian Ocean.

The Sutlej has its origins in Lake Manasarowar itself, although on occasion it draws its waters instead from the nearby Lake Rakas, which is situated at much the same altitude (4,475 metres). The river passes briefly through Tibet, then forces a path through the mountains of Himachal Pradesh (provinces of the snowy mountains, or Himalayas) and into the Punjab (five rivers), before joining with the Indus lower down in the plains.

Finally there is the Ganges, 'mother Ganga', the most sacred river of them all. It too can be regarded as rising in the Kailas region, this being the point of origin of its first major affluent, the Karnali, which itself is fed by the Humla-Karnali and crosses right through western Nepal. 'The waters of the Ganges bring liberation,' said Ma Ananda Moyi, and Shri Ramakrishna declared, 'The water of the Ganges is as pure as the Brahman.' Officially, of course, the source of the Ganges lies in Garhwal in Uttar Pradesh (the northern province). Here it receives the waters of local tributaries such as the Alaknanda, Bhagirathi and Yamuna, along which are situated many of the major pilgrimage centres, among them Kedarnath, Badrinath, Gangotri, Yamunotri, Hardwar and Prayag (Allahabad, City of God). The Ganges is further sanctified as it flows south-east through the holy city of Benares. By the time it has reached that point it has been swollen not only by the waters of the Karnali but also of the Kali Gandaki, on which lies Muktinath, visited by many pilgrims. This latter river changes its name when it reaches India – a common phenomenon; after uniting with the Marsyandi and the Trisuli, it becomes known as the Narayani. The Ganges itself is fed by the supremely holy waters of the Bagmati, the river of Kathmandu, on which lies the sacred Hindu site of Pashupatinath, and then by the Sapt Kosi, one of whose most famous tributaries is the Arun. Further down river, the Ganges is joined by the Mechi, which marks the frontier between India and Nepal and is itself fed by the Kankai. In a last grand gesture, the Ganges meets the Brahmaputra and flows majestically on to the Bay of Bengal, where the Mouths of the Ganges spread out into a vast delta.

So we can see that the Himalaya rivers actually cross over the great chain. Or to put it another way, Himalaya does not, as is often assumed, form a watershed. Most of the rivers have their point of origin on the far side of this imaginary demarcation line, most frequently in Tibet. This is certainly true of the Indus, Sutlej, Brahmaputra and Ganges. In view of the modest precipitation enjoyed by Tibet, this is a surprising fact. Scientists have not been slow in producing explanations, many of them contradictory.

One theory, which may be worth quoting, goes roughly as follows. It begins with a prayer written by the Bengali poet D. L. Roy: 'Oh! Mother India! the day on which you emerged from the blue ocean, what a day of ecstasy it was, what a day of joy.' According to the German geophysicist A. Wegener in 1915, some hundreds of millions of years ago the ancient continent split apart and divided into two separate sections. Between the now distinct land masses, the sea of Tethys was created. The two new continents were Angara, to the north, and Gondwana, to the south. The Deccan was a part of the southern land mass. Naturally the rivers of these two continents debouched into the newly formed sea, delivering onto its bed deposits of clay, mud and sand. The underlying earth's crust subsided under these deposits which, according to the geologist Toni Hagen, acquired in time a depth of a hundred or more kilometres.

These sizable deposits in the vast geosynclinal of the sea of Thetys are now to be found on the upper slopes of the principal peaks of Himalaya, notably on Qomolungma (or Everest), the highest peak in the world. What apparently caused this to happen is that the two continents began to draw nearer to each other, while at the same time the undersea trough, a weak point in the outer layer of the earth's crust, came under intense pressure from subterranean forces. The collision of the two enormous land masses and the volcanic eruptions deep under water caused the level of the bed of the Tibetan sea to be raised. Gradually, as the trough was filled in, a fold was formed; this eventually broke above the level of the waters, running like a scar from east to west. Ultimately it became a distinct ridge and grew, still along the same axis, into a chain of mountains even higher than the present-day Himalayas.

This titanic upheaval occurred some fifty million years ago. The argument among scientists today revolves around the question of the relative importance to be attached to the phenomenon of shifting continents, and that of the expulsion of viscous, incandescent matter from the earth's core. It is hardly for us to make a judgment, but all the same it is logical to assume that both processes contributed in some part to the exceptional altitude of the Himalayan peaks.

Whatever the precise details, the suggestion is that a narrow residual strip of sea still separated the Himalayas from the plateau of Deccan. The Thetys sea itself had apparently shrunk and was trapped to the north of the Himalayan barrier, towards the end of the Tertiary period. This is proved beyond all dispute by the discovery of recent and continuous deposits of sediment on the Tibetan plateaus. Other such deposits are to be found on the upper slopes of Everest, Cho Oyu and other mountains in the range, presumably the result of displacement of the Tibetan plate.

With the extension of he Aravalli Hills, running from the south-west to the north-east, along a line passing through Delhi and right up to Garhwal, the two bays of Sindh and Bengal came into being. As they gradually became blocked, they were replaced by a river, the Indobrahm, flowing east to west. When the Aravalli Hills in turn were elevated, this river split into the present-day Indus (Sindhu) and Ganges.

This orographical account supplies a basis for understanding the process by which Himalaya was formed, together with its great watercourses. Above all, it explains why the rivers have their sources on the far side of the great physical divide and not on the southernmost slopes. At one time all the channels drained directly into the sea of Thetys. When the upward thrust of central Himalaya began, the rivers eroded a path, retreating where necessary, and continued to force an exit through the newly elevated terrain. This, then, is the explanation for the massive gorges, the deepest in the world, the river valleys of the Indus in Ladakh, the Sutlej, the Kali Gandaki, the Arun, the Tista, and even the Tsangpo which, at the point where it bends sharply, loses more than 2,000 metres in altitude.

When one looks at the continent of Asia as a whole, it is immediately apparent that these rivers do not flow into the Arctic or the Pacific, but exclusively to the south. In addition, one notices several stretches where water must have accumulated at certain periods before the crossing of the Himalayan barrier. No doubt these mark the rivers' original points of destination. Such a hypothesis is supported by the presence of salt deposits in these spots. In Asia it is not unusual to come across rivers that are prevented by landscape relief from debouching into the sea. One such example is the Tarim in Central Asia, with its three tributaries, the Kashgar, Yarkand and Aksu.

Once the rivers have passed through the main Himalayan range and crossed the central valley, they immediately come up against another obstacle of lesser altitude, the Mahabharat. Before breaching this range, they trace a pattern of sinuous and winding loops, forming numerous lakes. It is as if they were pausing to take stock. They seem to draw themselves up in order to gather their strength and generate a surge of power before making the great leap to the most propitious spots. Once again, spectacular gorges cut deep into the Himalayan chain. These wounds mark the departure of mighty rivers towards the Ganges, the mother and provider of northern India.

Clearly there exists in Himalaya an enormous and untapped potential for hydro-electrical power. The conditions for exploiting this form of energy could hardly be more favourable: there are variations of level, strong currents, narrow gorges, reserves of water up-river, and suitable rock formations. Some dams already exist, such as the Mandi Dam (48 megawatts) erected by the British in 1935 in the Beas Valley, the region of Kulu which forms part of the Sutlej tributary system. There is also the Bhakra Dam, built after independence and one of the most important suppliers of power to the sub-continent. Even so, the present installations amount to very little when compared with the vast resources that could be exploited by Pakistan, India, Nepal, Sikkim and Bhutan. Being a renewable sources of power, the rivers surpass in importance the richest deposits of oil or coal, which are finite resources. It is baffling to see thousands of millions of human beings (if one includes the whole of Southern Asia) living and dying in extreme destitution when all around them there is wealth for the taking.

International organizations are beginning to take an interest, and indeed projects are already under way to develop these natural resources, particularly in India, Pakistan and Nepal. Of course, one cannot strictly compare investments such as these with similar schemes in the industrialized countries. Here the energy cannot be used where it is produced. Power has to be transported. This means agreements between states, always tricky to negotiate, and the construction of a whole network of power lines for high, medium and low voltage. In addition, many dams could be designed specifically for irrigation purposes. This alone could do much to improve the vegetable diet of the people, and would eventually give impetus to the development of agriculture-based food-processing industries.

As this leads us on to consider the human context of the mountain areas, it is worth stressing once again that Himalaya has always been more accessible than one might expect, whether to the passage of pilgrims, traders, soldiers, missionaries or simply inhabitants of the region, long accustomed to trek for weeks on end in order to gather provisions for their families or to dispose of their own produce.

It is also worth recalling that these high places have traditionally offered a secure refuge to migrants such as the Tibetans, who have moved away and settled in border areas like Ladakh, a natural extension of Tibet, or in the northern zones of Nepal, Sikkim and Bhutan – also Arunachal Pradesh (the NEFA), which has become the home of the Bhotias.

There have been population movements in the opposite direction, too – for example, the retreat of the inhabitants of the Indo-Gangetic plain back towards the high massifs, fleeing from warlike invasions or religous fanaticism. The effects of such demographic shifts are to be observed all along the Himalayas, in the west, Baltistan, Jammu and Kashmir, in Himachal or Uttar Pradesh, Nepal and Bhutan.

The complex network of valleys in Himalaya has functioned as a surprisingly effective system of communication. The mountains do not by any means form a monolithic barrier. We should at least note the principal trans-Himalayan routes, for example the Muzaffarabad in Pakistan, which crosses the Babusar pass at an altitude of 4,500 metres and leads on to Gilgit, Hunza and thence to Yarkand in Chinese Sinkiang, via the Mintaka pass at 4,709 metres above sea level.

There is also a route linking Srinagar (City of Shri, the happy woman, meaning Laksmi, wife of Vishnu) with Leh, capital of Ladakh, which passes over the Zoji La at 3,700 metres; it leads on again to Yarkand via the Karakoram pass (5,575 metres). The name means 'grey stones' and is of Mongolian origin, for Karakorum was Genghis Khan's Mongol capital. The pass is mentioned frequently in travel stories and accounts of explorations and journeys undertaken by missionaries and traders.

Equally well known are the pilgrims' paths followed by Hindus and Buddhists journeying to Mount Kailas and Lake Manasarowar. One of these goes from Simla over the Shipki pass (4,694 metres). The other two start in the Ganges delta and lead over either the Mana (5,456 metres) or the Niti pass (5,068 metres).

To the east lies the Gandaki route, which gives access to the Tsangpo and comes up from India via Mustang. To the east of that is a well established route, called the Chinese road to Nepal, which links Kathmandu and Shigatse, passing through Kodari.

Still further to the east, and the last on our list, is a very ancient track linking Darjeeling and Lhasa, passing through Kalimpong, Gangtok, the capital of Sikkim, the valley of Chumbi and Gyantse. It is this route that was followed by the first British expeditions to Everest.

Since the beginning of our century there has been an explosion of attempts to conquer the high peaks of Himalaya – fourteen of which, as mentioned earlier, rise to a height of over 8,000 metres. The early exploration of Himalaya was undertaken by expeditions of enormous size, organized like military columns. To some, these recalled a less peaceful occasion, when Colonel F. Younghusband led an army to Lhasa in 1904; the epic march was undertaken in order to show a British presence in Tibet at a time when the Tsarist Empire had designs on the area. Sir Francis Younghusband, as he became, won a great name for himself in the history of Asian exploration. He set up and often participated in many British expeditions to remote parts of Central Asia and Himalaya.

In the early days of the great Himalayan adventure it was regarded as essential to be motivated by a spirit of scientific enquiry. It seemed unthinkable to confess to climbing the mountains for their own sake. It was no different, of course, for Horace-Bénédict de Saussure when he climbed Mont Blanc in the late eighteenth century. The Alpine expeditions of that era always included a group of scientists whose mission it was to carry out research in meteorology, geology, cartography, botany, zoology, ethnology, etc. To make teams of this type operational in the inaccessible reaches of Himalaya, it was necessary to assemble veritable armies of men. This applied, for example, to the expedition led by the Duke of Abruzzi to the Karakoram in 1909, which included among its members a famous photographer called Vittoria Sella; to the expedition led by the Duke of Spoleto in 1928–29, in the same Baltoro region; and to the Italian expedition of 1973 to Everest led by G. Monzino, which comprised no fewer than 64 climbers, 100 sherpas, 2,000 porters, and 3 helicopters! It is true that the British teams of 1921, 1922 and 1923 had provided them with a precedent – but one that in their case was amply justified, since they had to skirt Nepal, to which entry was then strictly forbidden. The route they followed led to the east of Nepal, via Darjeeling and Kalimpong to the Chumbi valley, in Tibetan territory, and then west through Tibet proper. The size of these miniature armies always aroused considerable apprehension in the local populace, who had good cause to be wary. Because of the distance from base camp, usually at Darjeeling, it was essential to use large numbers of porters, horses and yaks. Other British expeditions followed, in 1933, 1935, 1936 and 1938, until at last Sir John Hunt's expedition of 1953 reached the summit of Everest itself. This was accomplished on the very day of the coronation of Queen Elizabeth by two members of the party, Sir

Edmund Hillary and the sirdar Sherpa Tenzing Norkay. An act of perfect symbolism, not only in its felicitous timing, but also because one of the climbers was a native of the region, and in making the ascent conquered his goddess, the mother of his world!

There is an anecdote attached to this, of particular poignancy to the French. In 1950 France was for the first time granted official permission to enter the kingdom of Nepal. Out of deference to the experience of the British, the present author proposed to his friends in the Alpine Club that they should be allowed another shot at the summit of the world. But the deal was that, if their expedition failed, they would raise no objections to an all-out attempt by the French. Meanwhile it was understood that the newcomers would tackle an 8,000-metre peak in order to familiarize themselves with Himalaya and its problems. This they did, by climbing Annapurna – the first of the 8,000-metre peaks to be conquered – in 1950.

Alas for the French, Everest was climbed in 1953, after a failed attempt by the Swiss with Raymond Lambert and Tenzing in 1952. The British success, which won them international acclaim, was of course celebrated in a friendly way by the two expeditions assembled a few months later in Paris.

The successful ascents of Annapurna and Everest marked the beginning of the heyday of Himalayan mountain exploration. In the course of the next twenty years all the 8,000-metre peaks were scaled. Today expeditions to Himalaya are at the rate of about thirty a year, a good proportion of these being Japanese. For the sake of completeness, we should perhaps mention among the large-scale expeditions those mounted by the Chinese, in particular that of Wang Fu-chu, who on 25 May 1960 (with 25 climbers and over 200 people to handle supplies alone) reached the summit of Everest and placed on it a statue of Mao Tse-tung, together with the five-starred flag. In 1975 there was another Chinese expedition with a massive military-style supply column. The most distinguished member of this party was a Madame Phanto, from Shigatse in Tibet, who became, by just a few days, the second woman to stand on the highest spot in the world – the first being the Japanese woman Junko Tabeï who reached the summit only a week earlier.

Since all the major victories had been won by 1970, attention turned to the peaks of 7,000 metres. The 8,000-metre climbs became the preserve of the climbing élite, who attempted the ascents either by different routes from those previously used, or in 'Alpine conditions', that is, in small teams roped together, often without oxygen and sometimes using solo climbers. Such was the ascent undertaken by the Tyrolean climber Rheinhold Messner, and the Japanese Y. Kato, who died shortly after reaching the summit of Everest.

The great era of Himalayan exploration would now seem to be drawing to its close, and climbing in Himalaya has become comparable to Alpinism in Europe. The difference is that virtually no virgin territory is left in the Alpine regions, whereas Himalaya offers immense possiblities in the way of unattempted climbs. There is still ample opportunity for reputations to be made.

It is difficult to understand the atmosphere in which these twentieth-century expeditions were undertaken without knowing something of the area's history. In Himalaya everything is interconnected, in space as well as time. We have briefly discussed the topography of the region, and said something about the peoples who have taken refuge there. But their history is inseparable from that of the countries adjacent to Himalaya.

As we know, in these high valleys much that is valuable from the past has been preserved – whether human types, religions, social structures or languages. It might be said that the great Himalayan range has been like a reef in an imaginary sea surrounding the mountains. Civilizations wash up against it, not to die but to deposit their most fundamental, permanent and precious attributes. The great heights of culture and historical achievement are rooted here. The mountain chain has always benefited, and still does, from being situated at the point of confrontation between different political, religious and military systems – even though these do not always come into open conflict, either because antagonisms die away or because they are biding their time.

Hinduism, and even more directly Brahmanism, evolved out of Vedism, the ancient religion of the Aryans. This ethnic group was concerned above all to preserve its racial purity. Politically, its members could not hope to maintain their dominant position and the resultant social privileges they enjoyed, since the aboriginal population outnumbered them many times over. They therefore pursued a policy of divide and rule, classifying the populace into rigidly separate categories. In this way the caste system came into being, justified and given divine sanction by a religion that was on the one hand monotheistic, in taking Brahma as its supreme deity, and on the other polytheistic, in its worship of Shiva, Vishnu and a whole pantheon of lesser gods and goddesses. It was not a revealed religion since there was no prophet who announced its truth to the world.

The point to be emphasized here is that the caste system, with the authority of a great religion behind it, became part of the fibre and being of the Indian people, and has remained so for thousands of years. According to the Hindu saga, man is made in the image of the cosmic logic and equilibrium. His membership of a caste is a function of the world order:

His mouth became the Brahman,
The warrior was the product of his arm,
His thighs were the artisan,
From his feet were born the servant.

According to this scheme, a man's moral worth and merits, assessed over a number of lifetimes, will decide the position he should occupy in the hierarchy. It was Hegel who stated that man is the sum of his actions, but even he did not think to extend that concept to previous lives or to the karma that controls a man's destiny – like a necklace onto which beads are threaded one by one. It is of course effectively impossible to rebel against such an immutable and God-given scheme. For us in the West, the novels of Rudyard Kipling give an excellent picture of the nobility and self-abnegation of the man who is ruled by his karma.

The first Indian Empire worthy of the name existed under the Mauryan dynasty, with its illustrious emperor Asoka. Three centuries before Asoka's accession Buddha was born, in Kapilavastu on the borders of Nepal and India, now Lumbini, and founded what is generally regarded as the religion of Buddhism – although it is more accurately a moral and philosophical system with a religious dimension. To the extent that it is a religion, it is a revealed faith, for it was announced to the world by a man of flesh and blood with no pretensions whatsoever to being divine – indeed he adamantly rejected any such claim. One recalls the story of the Buddha touching the earth with his fingers and calling on it to bear witness to the truth of his assertion.

This new and humane religion, characterized by a Franciscan compassion and tenderness, took hold initially in the Ganges plain. It preached serenity as an ideal, and was somewhat nihilistic in teaching a doctrine of renunciation. The great and enlightened ruler Asoka became an ardent proselytizer of the Buddhist faith, devoting all his efforts to spreading the religion to every part of India. In this he achieved notable success. But Hinduism was anchored in the hearts and traditions of the inhabitants of the sub-continent, and over the years it gradually won back lost ground, finally regaining a complete ascendancy. Often it simply subsumed Buddhist elements, thus strengthening its hold on the faithful. As there was never an open confrontation between the two religions, even at the start, this process of engulfment proceeded without difficulty. Traditional social organization provided an exceptionally effective bulwark against the egalitarian principles fundamental to Buddhism, by continuing to dictate an absolute discrimination between the castes. The role of women was highly specific and defined. And there remained an unbridgeable chasm between the higher castes and the untouchables, the pariahs, and the devotees of other religious faiths.

In the early years of this century Mahatma Gandhi enjoyed a position of enormous influence and power, and yet he failed completely in his intention of bringing about equality for all men. By this alone one can judge the strength of the obscure and deep-running forces that Hinduism could draw on to block an essentially humanitarian reform. It is not hard to see why Buddhism was obliged to give ground and expand its influence into other countries. Its doctrines were spread into most parts of Asia. Buddhism became the first universal religion, and in our own times it is still the faith with the largest number of adherents. In this respect Himalaya forms a religious frontier. As in the past, it is situated at the point where the faiths confront each other. Different modes of life survive in the different areas: polygamy in the southern ranges, polyandry in the northern zone. To the west, in Kashmir and the Punjab, the consolidation of Islam has set a natural boundary to the further spread of religions originating in the Ganges plain. In the east, in Assam and the NEFA, animism is still alive, although it can put up no more than a feeble resistance.

The original exploration and discovery of Himalaya is a fascinating subject in its own right. The ancient texts tell us that in 399 AD a Chinese pilgrim called Fa Hieng related terrifying tales of what had befallen him when he crossed the great chain. Safely back in his own country, he justified his adventures by declaring that 'no place is impenetrable for the man who is inspired by a sincere faith'.

Two other Chinese pilgrims are known to have journeyed through Himalaya in search of proofs of their faith – Hinan Tsang in 629, and Yi Tsing in 671. Hinan Tsong, a general of the Tang Emperor, crossed Sinkiang in 747 with an army of 10,000 soldiers and occupied Baltistan. Later it was the turn of the Jesuits, whose intention was to convert the Himalayan peoples and those of Asia in general. One of them was Antoine Monserrat, a Spanish Jesuit who lived around 1590 at the court of the Moghul Emperor Akbar. Akbar was tolerant of Christianity, and Monserrat was an exceptional man for his time. It is to him we owe the first map of Himalaya. To other Jesuits, this time French, we owe the first reference – in the seventeenth century – to Qomolungma, 'mother of the world'. In 1865 the British gave this peak the name Everest, in recognition of the services of the Surveyor General of India who acted as Superintendent of the Great Trigonometrical Survey (GTS). This efficient and tireless organization had been hard at work since 1800, sending out teams to make maps of the area. A geodetic survey based near Madras had established control points for triangulation throughout the whole Himalayan region. As a result of this programme it was established in 1852 that No. 15, situated in the forbidden kingdom of Nepal, was the highest of all the peaks.

To return to our account of Himalayan discoveries, in 1625 two Portuguese Fathers, Antonio Antrade and Manuel Marques, travelled over the mountains and founded a mission in western Tibet. Then came an era of military incursions, this time from the north. In 1792 a Chinese army crossed the high passes of Himalaya and overwhelmed the Gurkhas near Kathmandu. After about 1800, when Great Britain began to govern India, expeditions through the mountains became more frequent. Samuel Turner had already been sent on an embassy to Tibet in 1793, and in 1802–03 Francis Hamilton explored Nepal, as did J. B. Fraser shortly after him.

In 1812, disguised as Hindu pilgrims and using false names, Dr William Moorcroft and Captain Hyder Jung Hearsey travelled on yaks over the Niti Pass into Tibet. Once they had crossed the frontier they saw before them the wonder of Mount Kailas, about which they had heard so many tales. It was they who brought back the first accurate information about the region and, most notably, solved the mystery that shrouded the origins of the Ganges, Indus, Tsangpo and Sutlej rivers. They left enthralling accounts of their adventures, and in particular their encounters with the Gurkhas (Garhwal and Kumaon were part of Nepal until the First World War).

G. T. Vigne was one of many to explore Kashmir, as well as Ladakh and Baltistan, and in 1819 Moorcroft set out on a second expedition through the mountains to the same area. In 1829 a twenty-eight-year-old naturalist called Victor Jacquemont, a friend of Mérimée and Stendhal, was sent to Calcutta by the natural history museum in Paris. A cultivated and adventurous young man, he visited in turn Garhwal, Ladakh and finally Kashmir. The latter state was at that time ruled by a Maharajah of advanced years. The young scientist's charm won him friends everywhere. He made a triumphal entry into Lahore and was fêted and showered with gifts. He arranged to visit Srinagar, the Venice of India; he climbed to the Zoji La pass and discovered the Karakoram mountains, so high that they gave him vertigo and so glittering in the bright sunlight that he was temporarily blinded. The Maharajah was dazzled more by the young man than by the icy peaks and offered him the position of Viceroy of Kashmir, with the intention that he should shortly succeed to the throne. With infinite courtesy Jacquemont declined the flattering offer, using his scientific mission as his excuse. He took his farewell from the Maharajah and the assembled populace amid scenes of general lamentation. On his journey home he visited the Deccan before going on to Bombay, where he died in 1832. He was just thirty-one years old.

In 1848 the explorer and botanist Sir Joseph Dalton Hooker visited Nepal and then Sikkim. Soon after his arrival in the latter country he was arrested, and his release was secured only with great difficulty, following urgent diplomatic representations.

An expedition to explore the remote fastnesses of Himalaya was mounted around 1850 by the three Schlegintweit brothers, young German geographers. At the same time the first group of Alpine climbers penetrated the massif, fresh from a successful attempt on Mount Rose. They performed many daring ascents in Himalaya, notably in the west, but the expedition ended in disaster when one of the team was assassinated by a fanatic in Yarkand in 1857.

In order to establish the cartography of the forbidden regions, the GTS recruited and trained a number of the educated local people, known as pandits. In their pilgrim's staffs they concealed thermometers, which they immersed in boiling water and used to measure altitudes. Distances they estimated by counting the beads on their rosaries. One of the best known of these brave explorers was Nain Singh, whose first trip was to Lhasa. There were also Abdul Subhan and Ata Muhammed, who explored the gorges of the Indus; Hari Ram, who surveyed the hinterland of Everest in 1871; and Mirza Shuja, who was assassinated in Bukhara. Most famous of them all was without a doubt Kintup, a lepcha who was sold as a slave in Tibet around 1880 but managed to make his escape; he established that the Tsangpo and the Brahmaputra were in fact the same river, proof of which came only thirty years later.

After the area had been mapped, the great expeditionary period began. This divides naturally into a number of stages. First, the detailed reconnaissance of the mountains themselves; the early military-style expeditions; the conquest of the highest peaks; and finally, the ascents of the various faces and ridges using much smaller teams and at all seasons of the year.

Himalaya today remains a sacred place, where our existence recovers its meaning. The history of this 'third pole of the world' is a noble one, stretching far back in time, and it makes a powerful impression on anyone who goes there, to travel through its valleys and to inhabit its sanctuary of ideas and peoples.

A true journey is a mutation. Once marked by it, you can never be the same as you were before.

Captions

1   *Almond blossoms usher in the spring in Kashmir Valley (1500–2000 m) in mid-March. The winter snow can still be seen on the Pir Panjal mountains (+ 4500 m).*

2   *Mustard flowers ('sarson') carpet the Valley as the winter recedes to higher mountains. Poplars are still barren without leaves.*

3   *Poplars in late autumn sunlight, Dal lake, Srinagar.*

4   *The same poplars in summer; in the foreground, 'shikara', a typically long, slim boat used as a water-taxi in Dal lake.*

5   *Almond trees in bloom dotting a hill-slope near Pampore, Srinagar, and mustard flowers in foreground. Shepherds migrate to higher mountains as the snow-line recedes.*

6   *Caravan on the way to Margan pass (3610 m), leading to the upper Wardwan Valley from across Achhabal, south-east of Srinagar.*

7   *Crossing Mahagunas pass (4220 m), on the way to Amarnath Cave, where the annual pilgrimage takes place on the July–August full-moon day.*

8   *A meadow at Sonmarg (2670 m) in the evening. Sonmarg, at the foot of Thajiwas glacier, is easily the most picturesque spot in Kashmir Valley.*

9   *With the onset of spring, the Kashmir Valley stirs to life: women carrying baskets among almond trees on their way to Wular lake.*

10 *Winter scene, Tangmarg (2200 m), the base village for the ski-resort of Gulmarg.*

11 *Hazratbal mosque, Srinagar, with 'Chenar' trees (Platanus orientalis) in autumn colours. Hazratbal is to (Kashmiri) Muslims what Sarnath, near Varanasi, is to Buddhists. It is the sanctified repository of the Prophet's hair which was brought from Medina in AD 1692.*

12 *Autumn colours are seen at their most brilliant in the Kashmir Valley, starting the third week of October. In the foreground are walnut trees.*

13 *Sheep crossing a snow-bridge near the Amarnath Cave (3880 m). By September the shepherds leave the high pasturelands.*

14 *Children playing under huge 'Chenar' trees in autumn colours, Nishat Bagh, Srinagar.*

15 *Willows in early spring, with tender leaves about to sprout. Kashmiri willow makes excellent cricket bats and hockey sticks.*

16 *Solitary almond tree in bloom, below Shankaracharya Hill, Srinagar.*

17 *Manasbal lake (1590 m), which Francis Younghusband so rightly considered 'the supreme gem of all Kashmir lakes'. Lotus is nowhere more abundant or beautiful than on the margins of this lake during July and August.*

18 *On top of Margan pass (3610 m), looking towards Achhabal. Mountain passes are rarely covered with such sharp rocks and boulders; Margan is therefore easier to cross when covered with snow.*

19 *Sheshnag lake (3580 m), a midway halt for pilgrims on the way to Amarnath, as seen from the eastern ridge. Thousands of sheep graze on its fertile banks, and the mountains echo the barking of sheep-dogs.*

20 A typical Ladakhi settlement (c. 3500 m) on the way to Leh from Srinagar, before crossing the third and final pass, Fotu La (4095 m).

21 Lamayuru monastery (3520 m), below Fotu La, on the way to Leh. Lamayuru is the oldest monastery of Ladakh and is surrounded by the most unusual mountain-formations due to wind- and snow-erosion.

22 The fort dominates Leh (3520 m) like the Potala Palace of Lhasa, Tibet, but is much smaller and dilapidated compared to the Potala.

23 Young willows accentuate the barren sandy slopes of Ladakh, which makes one accept with conviction that Himalaya indeed rose from the sea.

24 Children in a school at Leh. Leh and its surrounding villages contain a considerable Muslim population in an otherwise Buddhist country.

Himachal Pradesh (Plates 25 to 36)

25 Buckwheat fields and the slate-roofed huts of Malana (3050 m), below Chandrakhani pass, Kulu Valley. The village has remained isolated from the mainstream of Kulu life and is anthropologically extremely interesting.

26 Children playing at Lari (3460 m), in Spiti Valley, with barley and potato fields in the background. Spiti can be translated as the 'middle country', because for years it has been a buffer region between the Indian hinterland and Tibet.

27 Solitary hut and fields at Sichling (3475 m), Spiti Valley. The tender green grass on the mountain slope is the only natural vegetation, found for three to four months in a year during summer.

28 View of Spiti river and fields of Ki village from Ki monastery (3960 m), the most important of five monasteries in the valley. It has a large collection of 'Thankhas' or painted and woven scrolls.

29 On the way to Mane lake (4510 m) one comes across the typically stark beauty of Spiti with its 'panorama of crags and rubble slopes that change their colours from pale pink to bright scarlet and from slate gray to deep blue and purple'. A 'churu', a cross between the cow of the plains and the Tibetan yak, can be seen.

30 'Earth tables' formed by the action of snow, extremes of temperature, and wind along the banks of Spiti, to be carried away eventually by rushing waters in summer, when the snow melts on the steep slopes.

31 A flock of goats on the banks of Chandra tal (4420 m), a high-altitude lake of Lahul, from where the Chandra river originates. It joins Bhaga to form Chandrabhaga or Chenab of the plains, one of the major tributaries of the Indus.

32 Sijling Gompa in Spiti on the way to Kaza, the District headquarters of Tabo. The lamas do their penance in such monasteries, which are located away from villages in sites which inspire the awe conducive to meditation.

33 Sheep returning to Kulu Valley for winter, from across Lahul, over the Rohtang pass (4420 m).

34 A boy from Khoksar (3140 m), Lahul. As one crosses the Rohtang, suddenly there is a marked change from the Aryan features of the natives of Kulu Valley to the Mongolian ones of those of Lahul.

35 Moonrise from Dharamshala (1500 m), as the setting sun lights up the Dhauladhar range near Kangra.

36 The Vajreshwari Devi temple at Kangra. Its riches and antiquity have been mentioned by historians and travellers as far back as the 11th century. In the background are the Dhauladhar mountains (4200–4800 m), which, together with the lovely plains of Kangra Valley, inspired the Kangra miniature paintings.

Garhwal-Almora (Plates 37 to 48)

37 Falls of the Bhagirathi river at Gangotri (3020 m). The river flows for a while in the northerly direction; hence the place is called 'Gangottari' or Gangotri – 'Ganga turned north'.

38 Entrance to Har-ki-dun (3570 m) – literal meaning, Valley of 'Hara' or Lord Shiva. The snow-mountain is an unnamed one near Borasu pass. Approached from Mussoorie, Har-ki-dun surpasses the famous Valley of Flowers in the beauty and richness of its flora.

39 Pilgrims in the courtyard of Gangotri temple. The temple is dedicated to the Ganga and is erected on the sacred stone where King Bhagirath is said to have worshipped Lord Shiva and the Ganga descended upon the earth.

40 Pilgrims on the way to Yamunotri (3185 m), traditionally considered the source of the Yamuna river. It is the westernmost of the four holy shrines of Garhwal Himalaya.

41 Fields of red buckwheat, Tons Valley, Garhwal. Just before harvesting, the multicoloured fields carpet the valleys between 2000 to 3000 m, in September and October, depending upon the height. Locally known as 'Chua', this forms the staple diet of people.

42 Kedarnath temple (3580 m) is the highest among the four Garhwal shrines which form the pilgrim circuit. Located at the foot of the mountain (6940 m) of the same name, the surrounding valley and the mountains have all the grandeur of Garhwal Himalaya, which Longstaff considered 'the most beautiful country of all High Asia'.

43 Dayaram, of Osla (2755 m) in Tons Valley, my young and enthusiastic guide for Har-ki-dun, with a bunch of fragrant 'jawai' (Primula Stuarti), which he had just discovered near a mountain stream.

44 A Garhwali child wondering at the ways of the 'alien' pilgrims from the plains of India, in his hamlet near Kedarnath.

45 Verditer flycatcher and plum blossoms, Kausani (1890 m), near Almora, in late March. As one travels eastwards from Kashmir, gradually the cherry, almond and peach disappear, in that order.

46 Kedarnath (6940 m) from Panwali ridge (3300 m), easily one of the best viewpoints of Garhwal Himalaya. Panwali is on the old pilgrim route, now in disuse, between Gangotri and Kedarnath, and its grassy slopes teem with alpine flowers during monsoon.

47 View of Bhagirathi peaks from Chirbas (3610 m), on the way to Gaumukh or the snout of Gangotri glacier. From left to right, Bhagirathi II (6510 m), Bhagirathi III (6450 m) and Bhagirathi I (6860 m). In the snow-mountains of Garhwal, Nepal and Sikkim, it is easier to decipher the very face of eternity than in the mountains of Karakoram, Kashmir or Himachal.

48 Nar Parbat (5860 m) from the Valley of Flowers (3700 m), as the swirling monsoon clouds unveil its cornices for a few minutes in the morning.

Nepal (Plates 49 to 67)

49 A woman typical of eastern Nepal in her ornaments and dress.

50 Open-air market near Dhankuta (1200 m), eastern Nepal. Villagers sell their produce in weekly markets, which are held on certain fixed days of the week.

51 The Indravati river (c. 1600 m), north-east of Kathmandu. Sandy islands of the river-bed keep changing every monsoon.

52 Everest massif rising from the valley of Imja Khola as seen from Thyangboche (3875 m). On the left, Everest (8848 m) peeps from behind Nuptse (7879 m) wall, while Lhotse (8511 m) can be seen on the right with its snow-plume.

53 Red and pink rhododendrons in bloom, Barapokhri (2980 m), central Nepal, with Lamjung Himal (6931 m) dominating the landscape.

54 Late autumn morning, Thyangboche monastery (3875 m). It commands the most magnificent view of the Himalayan giants like Everest, Lhotse, Nuptse, Kwangde, Tawache, Thamserku and Ama Dablam.

55 *An old sherpa at Mani Rimdu festival, which is celebrated at Thyangboche, usually on the full-moon day of November–December.*

56 *A sherpa from Khumjung (3780 m). Khumjung and Kunde are large twin-villages of Khumbu, typical of the sherpa way of life.*

57 *Approaching Kyangjin (3840 m), Langtang Valley, in early autumn. Situated north-west of Kathmandu, Langtang is popular among trekkers because of its accessibility and the spectacular views of Langtang Lirung (7246 m), Dorje Lakpa (6975 m) and other mountains and their glaciers.*

58 *One of the largest Buddhist stupas in the world, Bodhnath or the 'Lord of Wisdom', Kathmandu. The unblinking eyes of Lord Buddha look out at the world from all four sides.*

59 *Step-fields (c. 2000 m) north of Kathmandu, on the way to Helambu, testify to the hard work and ingenuity of Nepali farmers over thousands of years.*

60 *The famous sherpa village of Namche Bazar (3440 m), the administrative centre of Khumbu and the starting-point of many treks in the Everest region.*

61 *A girl from eastern Nepal.*

62 *Water-buffalo are quite common in the foothills of Nepal and are replaced by the cow, the 'Churu', and the yak as one ascends to mountain valleys bordering Tibet.*

63 *Gosaikund lake (4380 m), the largest of the cluster of high-altitude lakes in a basin to the west of Laurebina pass (4610 m), Central Nepal. Hindu and Buddhist pilgrims flock here on the August full-moon day.*

64 *The setting sun lights up Manaslu (8157 m), as seen from Barapokhri (2980 m), which also commands fine views of Lamjung Himal (6931 m), Peak 29 (7514 m), Himalchuli (7893 m) and Baudha (6672 m).*

65 *Huge pippal (Ficus religiosa) and bunyan (Ficus bengalensis) trees dot the Nepal countryside up to 1200 m. In a country where the majority travel on foot, these trees form ideal resting places for weary travellers.*

66 *The ridge nestling Lamapokhri (2835 m), a week's trek from Dharan bazar in eastern Nepal, has some of the best rhododendron slopes in Nepal Himalaya, and at the same time commands superb views of high mountains – Chamlang, Everest, Makalu and Kangchenjunga.*

67 *Thamserku (6608 m) is closest from the Japanese-built Hotel Everest View at Syangboche (3800 m).*

Sikkim and Darjeeling (Plates 68 to 77)

68 *Pine forest around Sandakphu, with rhododendron undergrowth, where the fierce winds, torrential rains and lightning have done their work.*

69 *Pemyangtse (2080 m) has glorious views of Sikkim Himalaya. From behind the fresh spring foliage can be seen, starting left, Little Kabru or Rathong (6679 m), Kabru (7338 m) in the centre, and Talung (7035 m). Behind Talung, on the extreme right, begins the ridge leading to Kangchenjunga.*

70 *The rising sun has just painted the trunks of dwarf rhododendrons, growing on the Singalila ridge near Sandakphu, and the moon is yet to set in the dark blue sky of high mountains.*

71 *A painting on the upper storey of the second oldest monastery in Sikkim at Pemyangtse.*

72 *A young initiate outside the main door of Pemyangtse monastery.*

73 *Patterns on a boulder in the bed of the Tista river, on the way to Gangtok from Darjeeling. Tista is the Ganga of Sikkim, draining the waters of the entire kingdom, and abounds in stones and boulders of exquisite hues and patterns.*

74 *After a snow-storm in early spring; view from Sandakphu (3630 m), two days' march from Darjeeling. Jannu (7710 m) is on the left and Kangchenjunga (8600 m) right centre. Also seen in front of Kangchenjunga, from the left, are Rathong (6679 m), Kabru (7338 m) and Talung (7035 m).*

75 *Fields (c. 1700 m) on the way to Rumtek monastery, opposite Gangtok, Sikkim.*

76 *Darjeeling (2307 m) is the home of tea, and tea-gardens cover the slopes up to 600–900 m towards the lower river valleys.*

77 *The stupendous character of the view from Sandakphu (3630 m) can only be appreciated when it is understood that the range seen has two groups of mountains, crowned by the highest and the third highest mountain on the earth's surface. From the left, Lhotse (8511 m), Everest (8848 m), Makalu (8420 m), and Chomolonzo (7815 m), with Makalu dominating in the setting sun. Singalila ridge is at the bottom.*

To the late Swami Anand,
a 'sadhu' in the noblest of Indian traditions,
who introduced me to Himalaya and
to the still greater realms of beatitude.

शान्ता महान्तो निवसन्ति सन्तो वसन्तवल्लोकहितं चरन्तः ।
तीर्णाः स्वयं भीमभवार्णवं जनानहेतुनान्यानपि तारयन्तः ॥

*There are saints, calm and great, who bring good to
others, quietly and unasked, as does the Spring.
They have already crossed the dreadful ocean of life
themselves and help others to cross it, spontaneously
and without any motive.*

Shankaracharya: *Vivekchudamani*, 39

2

4

6

8

15

22

23

27

30

38

43

44

53

58

61

71

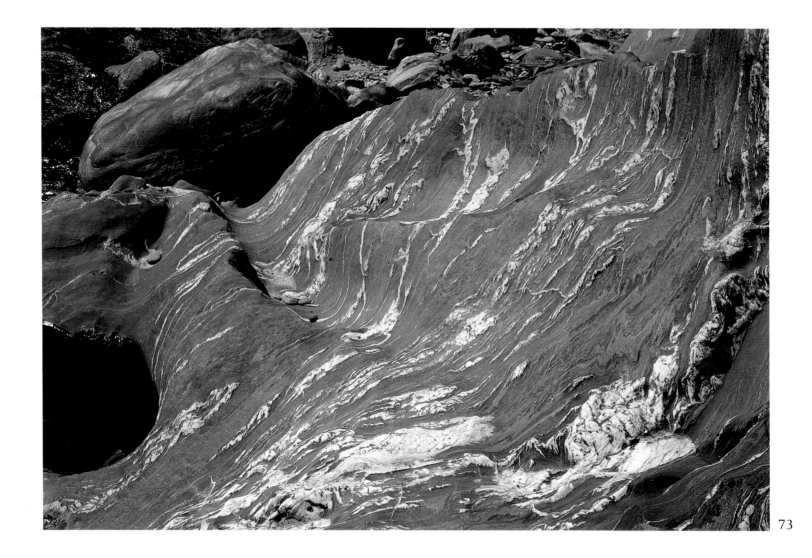